Go, Gorillas, Go

Fiona Kenshole

T0369614

Name _____

Age _____

Class _____

OXFORD
UNIVERSITY PRESS

OXFORD
UNIVERSITY PRESS

Great Clarendon Street, Oxford OX2 6DP

Oxford University Press is a department of the University of Oxford.
It furthers the University's objective of excellence in research, scholarship,
and education by publishing worldwide in

Oxford New York

Auckland Bangkok Buenos Aires Cape Town Chennai
Dar es Salaam Delhi Hong Kong Istanbul Karachi Kolkata
Kuala Lumpur Madrid Melbourne Mexico City Mumbai
Nairobi São Paulo Shanghai Taipei Tokyo Toronto

OXFORD and OXFORD ENGLISH are registered trade marks of
Oxford University Press in the UK and in certain other countries

ISBN-13: 978 0 19 440114 2

Printed in China

ACKNOWLEDGEMENTS

The publisher would like to thank the following for their kind permission to reproduce the following:
Alamy Stock Photo pp 2 (silverback/Martin Harvey), 8 (chimpanzee/louise murray), 12
(Viranga mountains/Steve Bloom Images), 22 (gorilla eating/Martin Harvey); Getty Images
p30 (man and gorilla/Martin Harvey); **Shutterstock** pp4 (gorilla reclining/James Laurie), 6
(orangutan/Sergey Uryadinkov), 10 (mountain gorilla), 14 (gorilla family/Fiona Ayerst), 16
(silverback/paula french), 18 (female gorilla/Eric Gevaert), 20 (young gorillas/M.Martinho),
24 (family of gorillas/Onyx9), 26 (gorilla yawning/KARI K), 28 (fierce silverback/FCG).
Cover courtesy of imageBROKER/Alamy Stock Photo
Illustrations by: Jackie Snider

With thanks to Sally Spray for her contribution to this series

Reading Dolphins
Notes for teachers & parents

📖 Using the book

1 Begin by looking at the first story page (page 2). Look at the picture and ask questions about it. Then read the story text under the picture with your students. **Use section 1 of the CD for this if possible.**

2 Teach and check the understanding of any new vocabulary. Note that some of the words are in the **Picture Dictionary** at the back of the book.

3 Now look at the activities on the right-hand page. Show the example to the students and instruct them to complete the activities. This may be done individually, in pairs, or as a class.

4 Do the same for the remaining pages of the book.

5 Retell the whole story more quickly, reinforcing the new vocabulary. **Section 2 of the CD can help with this.**

6 **If possible, listen to the expanded story (section 3 of the CD). The students should follow in their books.**

7 When the book is finished, use the **Picture Dictionary** to check that students understand and remember new vocabulary. **Section 4 of the CD can help with this.**

💿 Using the CD

The CD contains four sections.

1 The story told slowly, with pauses. Use this during the first reading. It may also be used for "Listen and repeat" activities at any point.

2 The story told at normal speed. This should be used once the students have read the book for the first time.

3 The expanded story. The story is told in a longer version. This will help the students understand English when it is spoken faster, as they will now know the story and the vocabulary.

4 Vocabulary. Each word in the **Picture Dictionary** is spoken and then used in a simple sentence.

Do you know who I am? You might not recognize me, but I'm one of your closest relatives. That's right, I'm a gorilla.

Let me show you around my world. Let's take a trip together and meet the rest of the family.

Complete. Use these words:

hand   shoulder   body   foot   head
leg   mouth   arm   eye   ear   knee   nose

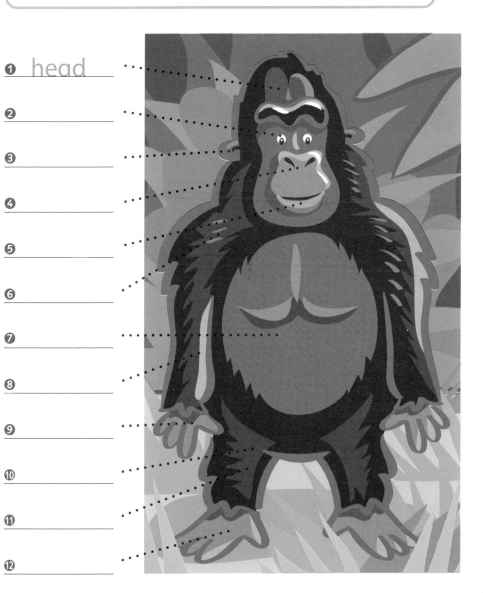

① head

② _____

③ _____

④ _____

⑤ _____

⑥ _____

⑦ _____

⑧ _____

⑨ _____

⑩ _____

⑪ _____

⑫ _____

I belong to the great ape family. We are
not monkeys. Monkeys have tails, but apes
do not. Apes all have long, strong arms.
We are intelligent, and we can do many
things that humans can do.

      Gorillas are not the only great apes.
Let me introduce you to the others.

Complete the sentences.

❶ Humans can walk on two legs, _and gorillas can walk on two legs, too_ .

❷ Humans can drive a car, _but gorillas cannot drive a car_ .

❸ Humans can cook food, _____

_____ .

❹ Humans can climb trees, _____

_____ .

❺ Humans live in families, _____

_____ .

❻ Humans can speak, _____

_____ .

❼ Humans like to sleep, _____

_____ .

In Southeast Asia, there's an ape called
the orangutan. The word orangutan means
forest person. Orangutans live in tropical
forests, and they live most of their lives
high in the trees. They use their long arms
to swing through the trees, looking for
fruit to eat.

Rearrange the words.

1 from Asia orangutans come

   Orangutans come from Asia.

2 big have they bodies heavy

_____

3 arms have short long they and legs

_____

4 in they most live their lives of trees

_____

5 not orangutans do tails have

_____

6 eat plants mostly orangutans fruit and

_____

7 gorillas are orangutans than smaller

_____

8 orangutans apes and gorillas are

_____

A smaller member of the ape family
is the chimpanzee. You can recognize
chimpanzees by their big ears, big eyes,
and cute face. They are really smart,
and good with their hands. They also
learn how to do new things easily.

Write about this chimpanzee.

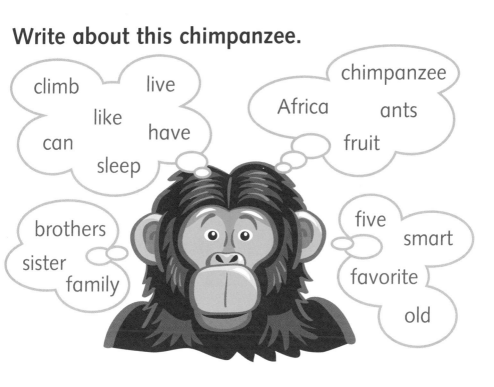

climb   live   like   have   can   sleep

chimpanzee   Africa   ants   fruit

brothers   sister   family

five   smart   favorite   old

Hello! I am Champ the _chimpanzee_.

I am _____ years _____ and I

_____ with my _____ in _____.

I _____ two _____ and one

_____. I am really _____,

and I _____ run and _____ trees.

I _____ to play and _____.

My _____ food is _____,

and I like _____, too.

Now we come to my family, the mountain gorillas. Like the chimpanzees, we live on the continent of Africa. We live right in the middle of the African rainforest. It's not too hot, because we live in some very high mountains.

1 Who are the gorilla's neighbors? Complete.

elephant

zebra

hippopotamus

giraffe

crocodile

lion

rhinoceros

❶ G I R A F F E
❷ [ ][ ][ ][ ][ ][O][ ][ ][ ][ ]
❸ [ ][ ][R][ ]
❹ [ ][I][ ][ ][ ][ ][ ]
❺ [ ][L][ ]
❻ [ ][ ][ ][ ][ ][ ][L][ ]
❼ [ ][ ][ ][ ][ ][A][ ]

2 Match the things we can see in Africa.

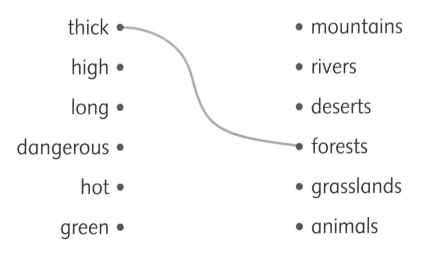

thick •   • mountains

high •   • rivers

long •   • deserts

dangerous •   • forests

hot •   • grasslands

green •   • animals

11

Welcome to my home. These are the Virunga Mountains. They are a great place for gorillas to live. These mountains are old volcanoes, and they are covered in thick forests with lots of good things to eat. They are very high, so the weather is cool and it rains a lot.

Put words from page 12 into this table.

Adjectives	Nouns	Verbs
great	home	welcome

We like to live in family groups. Usually, there are between five and ten gorillas in a family. We live together, and we eat together. We also travel through the mountains in a group, looking for food.

How many can you count in this family?

1 Read this story about a gorilla family.

My name is Nandi. There are six gorillas in my family. I have a grandmother, a mother and father, one brother, and one sister.

My grandmother is 32 years old. She is old and slow. My father is big and strong. He sometimes gets angry with us. My mother cares for us. My older brother likes to play tag with us. My younger sister is very cute. She likes to eat fruit and sleep. As a family, we do everything together.

2 Write a similar story about your family.

My name is _____

_____

_____

_____

_____

_____

The father of the family is called a
silverback because he has silver hair on his
back. He is the biggest gorilla in the family.
This silverback weighs 190 kilograms.
When he stands up, he is as tall as a man.

Check ☑ true or false.

	True	False
❶ A father gorilla is called a silverback.	✓	☐
❷ There are many big silverbacks in a family.	☐	☐
❸ The father gorilla is very heavy.	☐	☐
❹ The silverback gorilla is dangerous.	☐	☐
❺ Silverbacks are as tall as humans.	☐	☐
❻ The father gorilla is very strong.	☐	☐
❼ This silverback is in a tree.	☐	☐
❽ This silverback is walking through the grass.	☐	☐
❾ This silverback is walking on his hands and feet.	☐	☐
❿ This silverback has a baby on his back.	☐	☐

The other gorillas in the family are
females, young gorillas, and babies.

Here's a mother gorilla with her little
baby. The baby feeds on its mother's milk
for more than two years.

Soon the baby will learn to ride on its
mother's back.

Can you help the baby find its mother?
It must stay away from dangerous things.

fruit

crocodile

river

nest

elephant

rhinoceros

leaves

lion

snake

rhinoceros   hunter

What are these young gorillas doing? They are playing. They are having a lot of fun. Young gorillas like to play games, and many of these games help them to learn.

Gorillas become adults when they are about eleven years old.

What are these gorillas doing?

1 <u>These gorillas are</u>
   <u>playing.</u>

2 _____
   _____

3 _____
   _____

4 _____
   _____

5 _____
   _____

6 _____
   _____

7 _____
   _____

8 _____
   _____

21

Gorillas need to eat a lot of food every day. We eat flowers and leaves, and sometimes we need our strong teeth to get the best food out of the plants.

We also like to eat ants and worms. Gorillas love delicious fruit, but it's sometimes hard to find in the rainforest.

1 **What do gorillas eat?**
   Complete the crossword.

flowers

leaves   ants

worms

							T	
P								
L			V				
					B		

A N T S

plant
bulbs

F L | | | E | S | fruit | B |

| | | | H | | | K |

W | | | S | | F |

| | | | | | |

P | | | T | B | U | | B | |

| | | | | | |

seeds

tree
bark

plant
shoots

2 **Complete.**

Herbivores eat plants. Carnivores eat meat.
Omnivores eat plants and meat.

Humans are <u>omnivores</u>.

Zebras are _____.

Lions are _____.

Every day, we walk a long way to find
food. As we walk, we pick up food from
the ground. We also pick leaves and fruit
off the bushes and trees. I spend most of
the day eating, and when I'm not eating,
I'm resting. Each family has its favorite
places to look for food.

Circle the mistakes and rewrite correctly.

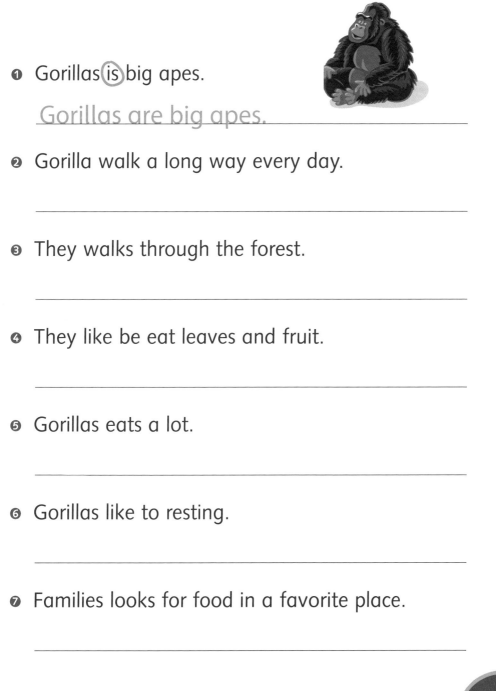

❶ Gorillas (is) big apes.

   Gorillas are big apes.

❷ Gorilla walk a long way every day.

   _____

❸ They walks through the forest.

   _____

❹ They like be eat leaves and fruit.

   _____

❺ Gorillas eats a lot.

   _____

❻ Gorillas like to resting.

   _____

❼ Families looks for food in a favorite place.

   _____

When night-time comes, we make nests to sleep in. Small gorillas make nests in trees, and big gorillas make nests out of grass and leaves.

We love sleeping so much. We even stop to sleep in the daytime.

Work it out.

❶ There are six gorillas in the group, but there are only five nests. Why?

<u>One gorilla is a baby.</u>

❷ The silverback is the oldest gorilla in the group. My mother is two years younger than him. I was born when my mother was 18 years old. I am now seven years old. How old is my father the silverback?

---

❸ If a gorilla spends six hours a day eating, four hours playing, two hours grooming to keep clean, and five hours walking, how long does it spend sleeping?

---

❹ The father gorilla weighs 180 kilograms. My mother weighs 90 kilograms. My grandmother weighs 85 kilograms. My brother weighs 72 kilograms. My baby sister weighs 59 kilograms. Our family weighs 554 kilograms all together. How much do I weigh?

What is this gorilla doing? He thinks that his family is in danger. He's standing up and showing his teeth.

Gorillas are usually peaceful animals, but when we have to, we stamp our feet and beat our chests. We scream and roar to protect our family.

Complete. Use these words:

> Africa   favorite   friends   hunters   life
> mountains   near   playing   studied   touched

Dian Fossey spent many years of her _life_
working with gorillas. She came from Kentucky
in the USA, but she worked in _____,
first in the Congo, and then in Rwanda.
She_____ the gorillas carefully, and
watched them eating, _____, and
sleeping. She also tried to protect them from
_____. She spent many hours in the
high _____ with the gorillas.
Sometimes they came very _____ to her, and
even _____ her. The gorillas became her
_____, and she was very unhappy
when her _____ gorilla, Digit, was
killed by hunters.

Some people hurt gorillas. They cut down the rainforest and so we have nowhere to live.

People and gorillas can live together, though. There are not many of us left, and we need your help. After all, we are one of your closest relatives.

Write eight interesting facts about apes.

1 _____

2 _____

3 _____

4 _____

5 _____

6 _____

7 _____

8 _____

Picture Dictionary

ant

forest

bark

fruit

bulb

gorilla

chimpanzee

grasslands

desert

knee

leaves

shoot

mountain

tail

nest

teeth

orangutan

volcano

seeds

worm

Dolphin Readers

Dolphin Readers are available at five levels, from Starter to 4.

The Dolphins series covers four major themes:

Grammar, Living Together, The World Around Us, Science and Nature.

For each theme, there are two titles at every level.

Activity Books are available for all Dolphins.

All Dolphins are available on audio CD.
(2 TITLES ON EACH CD 💿 SEE TABLE BELOW)

Teacher's Notes are available at **www.oup.com/elt/dolphins**

	Grammar	Living Together	The World Around Us	Science and Nature
Starter	• Silly Squirrel • Monkeying Around 💿	• My Family • A Day with Baby 💿	• Doctor, Doctor • Moving House 💿	• A Game of Shapes • Baby Animals 💿
Level 1	• Meet Molly • Where Is It? 💿	• Little Helpers • Jack the Hero 💿	• On Safari • Lost Kitten 💿	• Number Magic • How's the Weather? 💿
Level 2	• Double Trouble • Super Sam 💿	• Candy for Breakfast • Lost! 💿	• A Visit to the City • Matt's Mistake 💿	• Numbers, Numbers Everywhere • Circles and Squares 💿
Level 3	• Students in Space • What Did You Do Yesterday? 💿	• New Girl in School • Uncle Jerry's Great Idea 💿	• Just Like Mine • Wonderful Wild Animals 💿	• Things That Fly • Let's Go to the Rainforest 💿
Level 4	• The Tough Task • Yesterday, Today, and Tomorrow 💿	• We Won the Cup • Up and Down 💿	• Where People Live • City Girl, Country Boy 💿	• In the Ocean • Go, Gorillas, Go 💿